The "Law of Attraction" And The "Subconscious Mind"

Getting what you Want in Life!

The "Law of Attraction" And The "Subconscious Mind"

Getting what you Want in Life!

*The **$ecret** You Were Never Told About!!!*

A LANDMARK SELF-HELP BOOK

Information most readers never heard of Or new about!

Dr. Michael Williams, PhD, J.D.

iUniverse, Inc.
New York Bloomington

The "Law of Attraction" and the "Subconscious Mind"

iUniverse books may be ordered through booksellers or by contacting:

iUniverse
1663 Liberty Drive
Bloomington, IN 47403
www.iuniverse.com
1-800-Authors (1-800-288-4677)

ISBN: 978-1-4401-3709-9 (pbk)
ISBN: 978-1-4401-3710-5 (ebk)

Printed in the United States of America

iUniverse rev. date: 4/10/2009

The "Law of Attraction" And The "Subconscious Mind"

Table of Contents

Acknowledgments

I have written several books over the years but none quite as interesting as this. I want to acknowledge all the many great people down through the years and centuries that have explored and added to the study of the mind and to the "Law of Attraction." I have spent a number of years reading and researching these topics and have made some earth breaking revelation in my own life through these studies. There have been many great researchers and writers like Dr. Joe Vitale and they really have helped bring this valuable information to the public.

I want to thank my loving wife for all her support during the research and writing of this book. I also want to thank my wonderful parents Tom and May Williams for allowing me to explore and become whatever I wanted to become when I became and adult. My wife, father and mother were and are great people. The world would benefit greatly if there was more people like them.

Forward

During the writing of this book all I could think about was how to bring this information to the world at large in a format that was entertaining but also informative. This book holds information that was developed down through the years by many very bright and talented people.

If the reader of this book takes the time to really apply the principle outline in the chapters to follow they will see a change in their lives for the better. If they don't see a change for the better they are not applying the principle in the correct manner.

I want the reader to treat this book like and adventure, and adventure into their future wealth, love, and happiness. Read each chapter like they were opening a treasure chest and peering inside to see what the treasure holds for them. I wish and hope this material brings wealth, love, health, happiness, and abundance to everyone who reads it. Have fun on your new adventure.

This book addresses how and what the "Law of Attraction" really is and how it works from and physiological standpoint. Too many of the books written on the "Law of Attraction" only address what I call "The Wish List Perspective." I address how we perceive information, turn it into a desire, and how that through the conscious and subconscious mind we are able manifest our desires into existence through the "Law of Attraction."

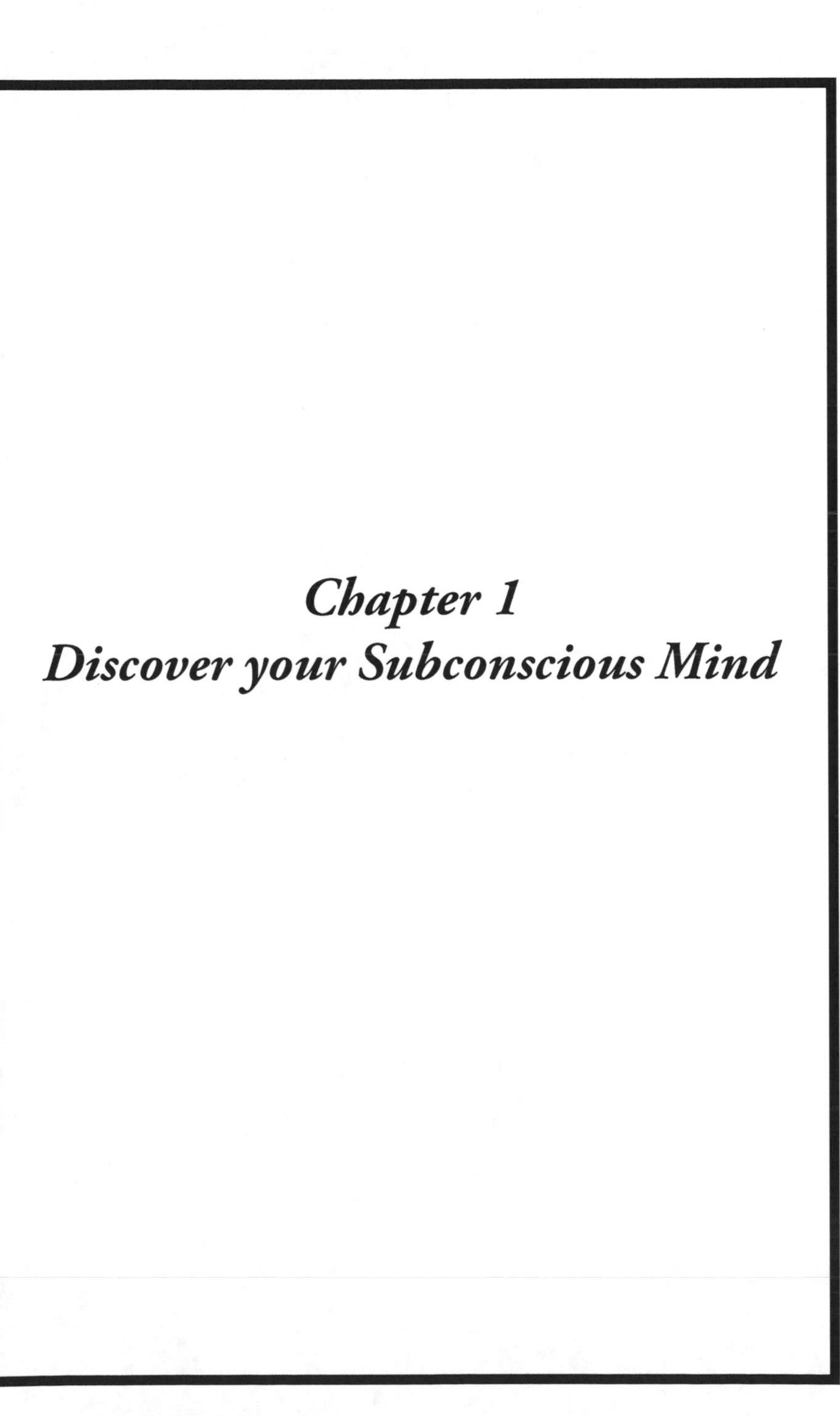

Chapter 1
Discover your Subconscious Mind

Why this book is different

One of the key differences of this book verses others on the topic of the "Law of Attraction" is:

- I have kept this book short and to the point and tried to cut out the fluff from other books on this subject that are 300 pages long. If you are like me I don't have the time to wade through a long book.
- I have included the subconscious mind as part of the subject matter. The subconscious mind is and integral part of the "Law of Attraction," and I have not found another book on the "law of Attraction" that truly addresses it.
- I am not only informing you of the concepts of the Subconscious mind and the "Law of Attraction" I am also showing you concrete steps to apply the techniques to gain what you want in life.

The Jeanie in the Bottle

You mind is all powerful whether or not you believe it. The mind has abilities beyond your imagination. Most people have know idea what their minds can perform for them and the riches it can bring them and there families. There is a storehouse of information within you, and by accessing this storehouse of information you can live life abundantly and joyously. It's like having a Jeanie in the bottle (your mind) at your finger tips all the time.

Most people are closed off to there subconscious mind and what great abilities they have within themselves. It is really surprising how many people don't even understand the basic concepts of how the subconscious mind works and that they even have a subconscious mind at all.

Within the world there are two types of people:

- People who attract what they want!
- And those who don't!
  It's just that simple, believe it or not.

The people that have this ability to attract what they want in life are using there subconscious mind and the Law of Attraction. Unfortunately the rest of the people of the world don't, and then they wonder why they are unlucky or worse they become vengeful or jealous of the people who have these abilities. Most people gain the ability to attract what they want in life through childhood experiences and the same holds true for not being able to attract what they want in life. Our thought patterns are influenced by our parents, friends, TV, movies, games we play the education systems we are exposed too and any other outside stimuli that reaches our conscious and then our subconscious mind. As we mature and become adults we have the ability to allow, or not to allow, this information to influence our lives and enter our conscious and then our subconscious mind.

Power of your Subconscious Mind

There are techniques presented in this book on how to contact and release the hidden power of your subconscious mind, you will have the ability to bring more wealth, power, health, and more happiness into you life, more than you ever thought possible. You will be inspired by a new light in your life. Through this light you will generate new forces that will enable you to bring into existence your hopes and dreams and make most of them come true. Most people don't realize that within there subconscious mind lays infinite power and wisdom to accomplish whatever they put there mind to. The subconscious mind is always there waiting for you to give it instructions on which way to lead. If you take the time now to recognize that within your subconscious mind awaits the deep thoughts necessary to take any form you desire in the world. Provided that you are open-minded to these possibilities, and if you are, your subconscious mind will reveal to you everything you want to know at any moment in time. Your subconscious mind will bring forth new ideas, new inventions, and new ways of looking at any given problem or issue. Most people have no idea of what there subconscious mind can provide them. The subconscious mind provides ways of dealing with any situation you may find yourself.

Through the wisdom of your subconscious mind you can and will attract the ideal companion as well as the right business to go into along with the right business associates that will support your business vision. The subconscious mind can show how to find the money you need, which in turn, will give you the financial freedom you want in life. Once you have mastered the principles of the subconscious mind it is exciting to have your life be so liberated and your future so promising.

Most people to don't realize that it's there right to discover the inner workings of there subconscious mind, and through this process find love, light, financial freedom, and happiness. The forces of the subconscious mind though invisible, are very mighty. One does not realize the power they have at any given time just waiting to be called upon. Once you learn to draw on these powers, it's incredible, you will actually become in possession of the power and the wisdom to further your ability to gather great abundance, joy, security, and dominion over your life.

The "Law of Attraction" ties directly to and aligns itself with the desires of your conscious and subconscious mind. When your conscious mind locks onto a desire and can hold that desire for any length of time it conveys that desire to the subconscious mind. In turn produces the vibrational energy needed through the "Law of Attraction" to bring that desire into existence. The longer you can hold that desire in your conscious mind the greater that given desire will be transferred to your subconscious mind. The same holds true for the "Law of Attraction." We will cover more on the Law of Attraction later in this book.

The power of the subconscious mind can lift people up out of a crippled state, make them whole both mentally and physically, and make them strong once again. Their subconscious mind gives them the ability to be free and be able to go out into the world and experience adventure, health and happiness. The subconscious mind has the ability to heal a troubled mind and broken body.

There are several good books on the subject of the subconscious mind on the market today and any serious individual that's wants the complete benefit of totally mastering there ability to control their subconscious mind needs to continue with their studies in this area. It's is fascinating to see all that science has discovered in the past 15 years in this area. So please continue your investigation and studies on this topic.

Chapter 2
How Your Subconscious Mind Works

Subconscious Mind Basics

If you want to make progress in any field of endeavor you need to learn the basics. Learning how to take information into your conscious mind, and then having the ability to move this information from your conscious mind to your subconscious mind take education and practice.

Before you can become skilled in this operation you must first understand the principles. Once you obtain the skills necessary you can practice its powers knowing the results you will receive. You will have the ability to apply these powers for definite and specific purposes and for any goals you may want to set for current or future accomplishments.

What most people don't realize is the Law of your mind is the Law of belief. What this means is to have the ability to believe in the way your mind works and you will need to believe in belief itself. What this means is the belief of your mind is the thoughts of your mind just that and nothing else. Any and all experiences are produced by your subconscious mind in reaction to your thoughts. You have to understand it's not the things you believe in, but the belief in your own mind that brings about your mental and physical results.

Fill your mind with health, wealth, and good thoughts, and you will start to see wonders happening in your life. Sometimes it will almost seem like magic what you subconscious mind can accomplish.

The Minds Duality

You need to remember this. Each person has only one brain, but the brain has two distinct and different functional parts. These two different parts of the brain have there own specific and distinct separate functions and these functions view the world differently from each other.

The names of these two parts of the brain have differed over the years. Some call these two parts of the brain the "conscious" and "subconscious" others call it "objective" and the "subjective", and others call it the "waking" and "sleeping" mind. There are several other names for these two parts of the brain but this is not a text book in medical school. So we will leave it at the definitions we just used. Whatever the names used their implications are the recognition of the brains essential duality. Throughout this text I use the terms "conscious" and "subconscious" to represent the duality of the human brain.

Conscious and Subconscious Mind

One way to start understanding the way your brain or mind works is to look at a forest. The forest represents your brain or mind, and within the forest stands thousands of trees which represent your conscious thoughts and hanging from the trees are seeds, and these seeds are your subconscious thoughts. When these seeds drop from the trees and find there way to the fertile ground below your thoughts are moving from your conscious to your subconscious and within the subconscious these thoughts take root. These subconscious thoughts guide the way you see and interact with the outside world.

Begin now to sow thoughts of happiness, joy, love, peace, prosperity, and action. Go someplace that is quiet and with no distractions, if possible, and think with conviction over these qualities. By doing this you will be able to accept these thoughts fully into your subconscious mind. Repeat over and over again, in this quiet state, whatever you want to come into your life. The more you visualize and repeat your desires to you subconscious mind the faster it will come into existence. These actions will continually plant wonderful seeds of thought in the forest of your mind.

When the brain or mind thinks correctly and when you start understanding these truths, and when these thoughts you have deposited in your subconscious mind are harmonious, constructive, and peaceful, then the real magic starts to begin and your subconscious mind will respond.

It's a shame that the majority of the world's population does not understand these principles. This world would be a much happier place if they did. Once you begin to understand these thought processes and how your subconscious mind works you can apply these powers to any problem or issue that may come up in your life. You will be amazed at what you will be able to accomplish, again it almost seems like magic.

If you look around at most of your family, associates, and the people in the world at large, most of them live in a world "*without.*" Now if you are one of the lucky people that are more enlightened and understand the principles of the subconscious mind you realize that the world without comes from within. When you start to visualize your thoughts you create and energy and vibration and when this vibrational energy of your desires match, these thoughts will materialize.

It will take some practice, but once you learn the truth about the interactions of your mind and how the conscious and subconscious play off each other you will be able to transform your whole life. If you want to change external conditions you must change the cause that brought on these conditions. Many continuously fail to see that the "*cause*" is what put them in their condition in the first place. To many people try to wrap long explanations around their conditions and can't see the forest through the trees. When you change the "*cause*" you change the "*condition or effect*". The Law of "*cause*" and "*effect*" it's just that simple.

What most people of the world do not understand is that we live in and unfathomable sea of infinite spiritual and material riches. You need to take the time and realize your subconscious mind is very sensitive to the conscious thoughts provided it. Those conscious thoughts form the foundation through which infinite wisdom, intelligence, vibrational energy, and vital forces of your subconscious mind flow. By directing your foundational thoughts in the direction you want to go, your infinite energy within you will bring on great benefits.

Most of the world's great men and women, in the past and present, held and hold and understanding of how the conscious and subconscious mind works and how it works in there favor. This gives them there great abilities to accomplish whatever they put there mind too. Yes, you too can have these abilities once you apply the principles in this book.

One key thing to remember when applying these principles, when you hold negative or irrational thoughts you block your subconscious mind from developing and delivering great ideas, emotional stability, the ability to take mountain moving action, and the greatest problem of all, it blocks your vibrational energy from being released from your conscious and subconscious mind, which in turn, blocks the Law of Attraction.

One of the most important points to remember is that if your conscious mind take a piece of information in and then conveys this information to your subconscious mind and your subconscious mind accepts this information, true or not, it begins to execute it. It's and unfortunate truth, and a subtle one at that, the Law of the Subconscious mind works for good and bad alike. This Law when applied negatively is the cause of most people's grief and failure in life. But when you think continues positive, constructive, harmonious thoughts you experience prosperity, success and health. Once you start thinking in this manner you will have peace of mind and a healthy body which are inevitable once you begin and stay the course.

The Subconscious just takes orders

The subconscious mind works a lot like a sponge. If you throw a sponge on something wet it just sucks it up. It makes no difference to the sponge that it's water or bleach. Here is another example. The subconscious mind is like a private in the army, the private doe not care if the order to charge the enemy is from a Major or a General, all the private knows is that he has been ordered to change, and charge he does.

This is how the subconscious mind works. It makes no distinction of whether to do something good or bad, right or wrong, smart or stupid, all it knows is to take action of some form. So it is vitally important to control your thoughts. Most people will ask do I have to monitor all the thoughts going through my mind? A resounding **NO !!!** unless you're a complete blank slate. Your previous mental programming should provide you with a certain amount of self preservation and you should already hold knowledge of right and wrong.

If you repeatedly tell yourself "I can't do it" your subconscious mind will take you at your word. Your subconscious mind will make sure that you can't accomplish whatever you are trying as long as you keep on telling yourself "I can't do it," take my word for it, you won't. You will go through life experiencing failure after failure and you will believe your circumstances made it so. Most people do not realize that they created these circumstances themselves by their own negative denying thoughts. Remember that the "Law of Life" is the "Law of Belief". If you believe you can, you can, and you will go on to accomplish more than you can imagine.

Chapter Review

1. The true treasure house for your future is within you. Look within for the answers to all your hearts desires.

2. Your subconscious mind holds all the answers to all your problems. If you make a suggestion to your subconscious mind before you go to sleep, your subconscious mind will work on this suggestion throughout the night, and when you wake in the morning, 8 times out of 10 you will have some kind of answer. Take time to listen to this answer before it slips away after you wake.

3. Remember that every thought is a cause, and every resulting condition and effect.

4. You subconscious mind is like a sponge, it does not no right from wrong, or good from bad. Think of positive motivating thoughts, and remember to visualize these thoughts; they give more meaning to your subconscious.

5. Never use expressions like "I can't do this" or " I will never amount to anything" you subconscious mind takes you at your word every time.

Notes

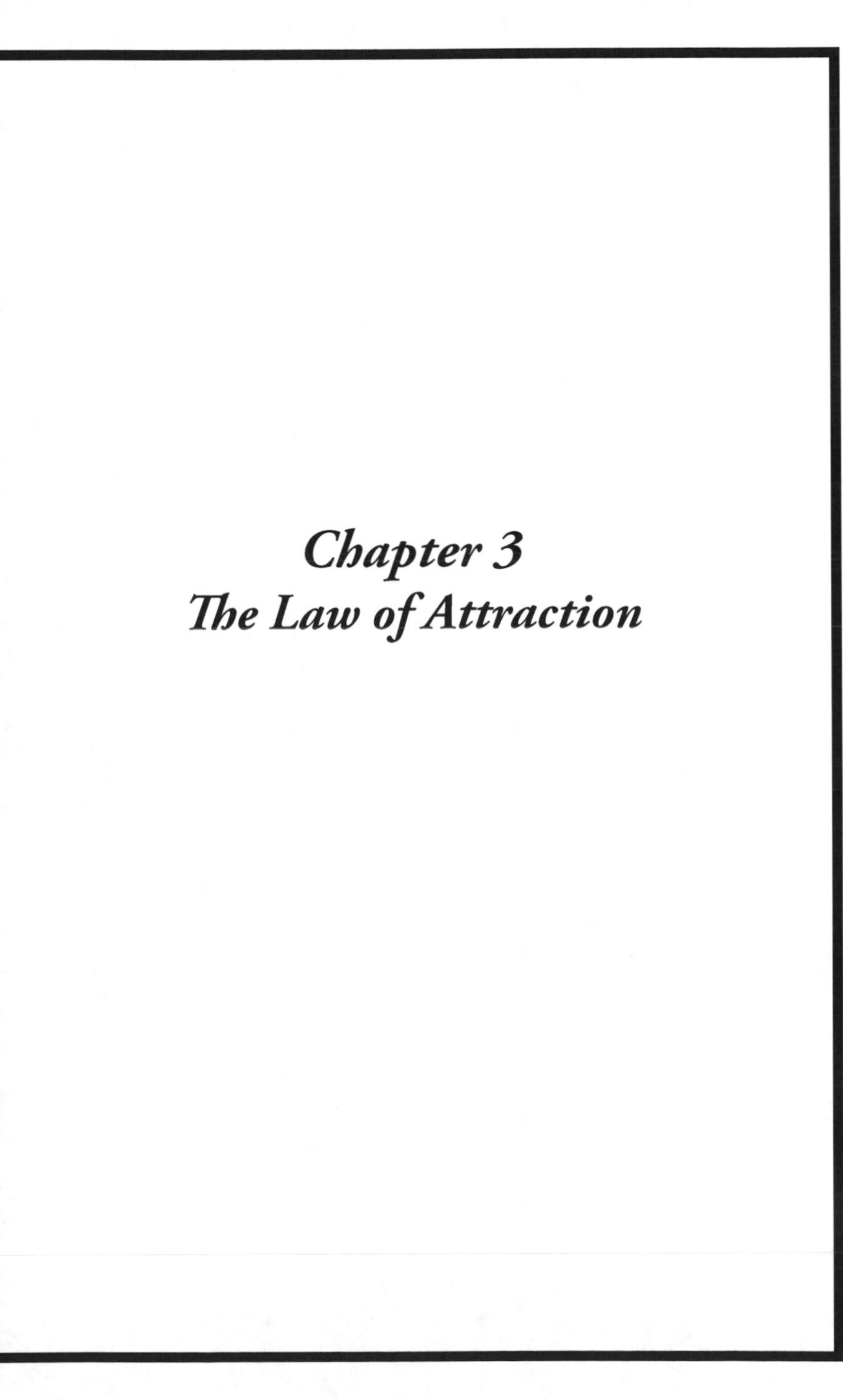

Chapter 3
The Law of Attraction

What is the Law of Attraction?

Most people have not either heard of the "Law of Attraction," or they have heard of it, but don't understand it. I have spent years learning and perfecting my ability to use the "Law of Attraction" but don't let this scare you away from using this incredible Law. You can put the "Law of Attraction" to work for you at any time anywhere. Right from when you first learn the basic principles of the "Law of Attraction."

A basic definition of the "Law of Attraction" is the ability to draw whatever you want in life to you whenever or wherever you want. I attract into my life whatever I give my attention, focus, and energy, good or bad. It may not manifest itself right then and there, but if you apply the principles of the "Law of Attraction" correctly whatever you want will manifest itself in time. It may happen in 1 minute or take 5 weeks or longer, but it will happen. You can't **rush** this "**LAW**."

Basic History of the "Law of Attraction"

Many people have heard of the "Law of Attraction" either from the media or through someone they know. In recent times the "Law of Attraction" was started being documented the early 1900s by different people.

- Atkinson, William Walter – 1906
  Thought Vibration or the Law of Attraction in the Thought World
- Holmes, Ernest – 1926
  Basic Ideas of Science of the Mind
- Holliwell, Dr. Raymond – 1949
  Working with the Law

Jerry and Ester Hicks were some of the early pioneers in the field of the "Law of Attraction," and early in the 1900s they made information and the teachings of the "Law of Attraction" widely available to the public.

Jerry & Ester Hicks Web Site: www.abraham-hicks.com for all their current teachings and additional information.

In the 1990s many articles and books started to appear on the market written about the "Law of Attraction," and its subject matter and appeal has grown to a much broader audience since.

You're Already working with the "LAW of ATTRACTION"

Have you even been at home or work and you have a thought that just pops into head, and then you notice at the very moment what you need just falls into place or comes to you from nowhere. Or you run into a friend that you were thinking about on the street or that friend gives you a call. All these experiences are evidence of the "Law of Attraction" at work in your life.

People use many expressions to describe the "Law of Attraction" in there daily lives. Below is a list of words used to describe this:

Karma	Luck	fate	Serendipity
Coincidence	It just fell in place		Out of the blue
It just came to me			I just thought of that

In this book you will learn to use the "Law of Attraction" more deliberately. You will gain the ability to attract and have and do whatever you desire in life.

The Science behind the "Law of Attraction"

What most people don't realize is there is a physiological foundation working behind the scene which creates our ability to have either positive or negative emotional responses to either internal or external stimuli. These responses drive one-to-one relationship with the "Law of Attraction."

There are many forms of energy in the universe: thermal, kinetic, atomic, electromagnetic, and potential, and what most people don't know is that energy can never be created nor destroyed. All forms of energy and matter are made of atoms, and each atom has a nucleus, and within this nucleus contains protons and neutrons around which orbit electrons.

Within the atom the electrons always orbit the nucleus in perfectly prescribed orbit or energy level that assures the atoms stability. Electrons can move into a higher orbit if acted upon by and outside energy source, and they can move to a lower orbit when they give off energy. When it comes to "Vibrational Energy" if atoms are aligned they will create what is called a "motive of force," all pulling together in the same direction. What this information is telling you is that if physical laws that can be observed and quantified in one area of science, there are most assuredly similar laws in other areas, even if science can't quantify them at this time in a lab.

What this explains is the "Law of Attraction" is not some new-age term or something being made-up just to sell books. The "Law of Attraction" is a real physical law of nature that every atom of your body and mind is constantly responding to which you can apply to create joy, happiness, and prosperity in your daily life.

Positive and Negative Vibrations

One of the key things to remember when dealing with the "Law of Attraction" is that each and every atom in your body and all the way throughout the Universe, everything has a vibrational level and everything emits vibrational energy. In the physical world there are only two distinct kinds of vibrations, "Positive (+)" and "Negative (-)." Every emotion or feeling, good or bad, causes you to emit or send-out vibrations to the world around you. Whether we realize it or not all of us send out either negative or positive vibrations. In fact each of us are always sending out vibrations. There is and old saying, "He gives off good vibes," well this is your ability to detect the vibrations this individual is giving off to the world around them. This detection is picked up, in most cases, through your subconscious mind. This ties the Subconscious mind, Vibrational energy, and the "Law of Attraction" all together.

At this very moment your mood or feeling is sending out vibrations to the world around you. By emitting these vibrations someone, somewhere will be in tune to your vibrations and pick them up in one form or another. The vibrations you are sending out maybe attraction for and individual in the next room, and the next thing you know that individual is engaging you in conversation. It happens more then you may think.

Here is where the "Law of Attraction" comes into play. The "Law of Attraction" is obeying the laws of physics and is responding to the vibrational energy you are sending out or offering this individual. This vibrational energy aligns itself with what your desires are, giving you more of the same, good or bad, positive or negative. For example, let's say it's

Friday morning and you are just getting out of bed and you feel great. The weekend is just around the corner, you have big plans for the weekend and you are meeting a good friend for breakfast. At that point in time you are sending out positive vibrations to the world. While you are is sending out these positive vibrations the "Law of Attraction" is responding, matching the vibrations you are sending out and providing you with more of the same. Remember, the "Law of Attraction" will always match your vibrational energy with more of the same, positive or negative.

So this individual gets out of bed pets the dog looks out the window and see a beautiful sunny day and then finds themselves saying, "what a wonderful day."

Next you have a person that is in a bad mood from the moment they got out of bed that morning. They go into the business office, yell at there administrative assistant, and go into their personal office. Then out of nowhere a client calls and cancels there contract with the company. Then they catch themselves saying "I should not have come into work today."

As you see, in both cases the "Law of Attraction" is at work. Their vibrational energy is orchestrating their outcomes, providing them more of the same.

Throughout this book we will identify the vibrational energy you are sending out and be able to make a clear conscious choice of whether or not you want to keep sending out these vibrations or change them.

Non-Deliberate side of the "Law of Attraction"

You will find that most people attract several things into there lives they don't want or need and they are curious about why they keep attracting these same unwanted things into their lives, over and over, again and again.

The reason this keeps on happening to people is:

What you think about most,

is what comes to them through the

"LAW OF ATTRACTION."

It is scary what people draw into there lives through their thought processes and the "Law of Attraction," and this does not stop with you conscious thoughts either. As was stated in and earlier chapter if we take something into our conscious thoughts and hold it long enough, or repeat this thought enough times, our subconscious mind will pick up on this thought and begin to work on it. Once the subconscious mind launches into action it will activate the "Law of Attraction" whether you want it to or not.

If you keep thinking bad thoughts, and giving off this bad vibrational energy, your subconscious mind will pick up on this, and again, activate the "Law of Attraction" and bring whatever you had been thinking about into your life.

People need to learn to focus their thoughts in a positive direction. I know at times this is difficult and most people feel it impossible but they are wrong. It just takes time to move your thoughts from negative to positive. Just remember Baby-Steps when trying to move your thought to the positive side of the spectrum. Start out slowly, each day take some time to focus your thoughts on something positive you want in life. Be it material or emotional. Over time you will find it easier to maintain these positive thoughts and the next thing you know what you were focusing on has materialized in your life.

People need to Reset their Vibrations

What most people don't realize is that at every moment in time we are sending out vibratinal energy. These vibrations are either positive or negative and by identifying the feelings you are experiencing, if negative, you can change those feelings to a positive state, which in turn will change the vibrations you are sending out. Remember there are only two kinds of vibrational energy: Positive and Negative.

Any person can reset their vibrational energy at any time from negative to positive by simply choosing different thoughts and words. It's as easy as asking yourself "what do I want?" Another key fact to remember is that you can only send out one vibration at a time. So by changing your thoughts you change the vibrations being sent out and at that point you have reset your vibrational energy. The "Law of Attraction" does not have a memory or remember the vibrations you sent out 10 minutes ago, 2 days ago, or 10 weeks ago. It will only respond to your current vibrations, and the vibrational energy being produced at the very instance and bringing you more of the same.

In the next chapter "Getting what you Want !!!" I will provide you with techniques that will bring wealth and emotional happiness into your life if you apply the principle in these techniques on a regular basis.

Chapter review

1. What is the "Law of Attraction?"

A basic definition of the "Law of Attraction" is the ability to draw whatever you want in life to you whenever or wherever you want. I attract to my life whatever I give my attention, focus, and energy to, good or bad.

2. The Science behind the "Law of Attraction."

What most people don't realize is there is a physiological foundation working behind the scenes which creates our ability to have either positive or negative emotional response to either internal or external stimuli. These responses drive one-to-one relationship with the "Law of Attraction."

3. Positive and Negative Vibrations

One of the key things to remember when dealing with the "Law of Attraction" is that each and every atom in your body and all the way throughout the Universe, everything has a vibrational level, and everything emits vibrational energy. In the vibrational world there are only two distinct kinds of vibrations, "Positive (+)" and "Negative (-)." Every emotion or felling, good or bad, causes you to emit or send-out vibrations to the world around you.

4. **Non-Deliberate side of the "Law of Attraction"**

You will find that most people attract several things into there lives they don't want or need, and they are curious about why they keep attracting these same unwanted thing in their lives over and over, and again and again. The reason this keeps on happening to people is:

What you think about most,

is what comes to them through the "LAW OF ATTRACTION."

5. **People need to "Reset" their Vibrations**

   Any person can reset their vibrational energy at any time from negative to positive by simply choosing different thoughts and words. It's as easy as asking yourself "what do I want?"

Notes

Chapter 4
10 Techniques to get What you WANT in Life!!!

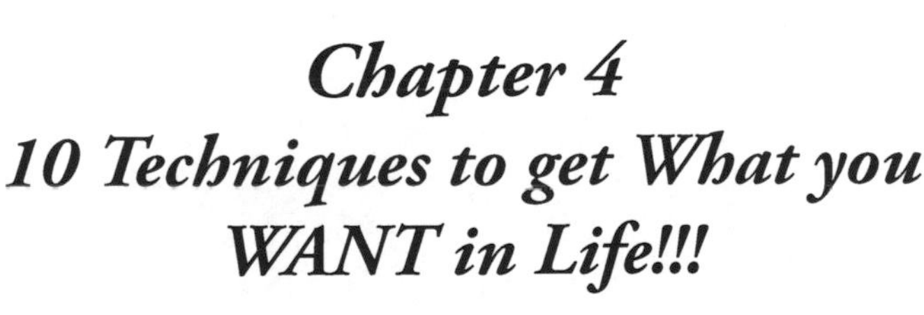

Manifesting what you want

What I am going to present to you in this chapter are techniques to bring about the manifestation of your wants and desires in life. So many people today wish they could experience financial abundance in their lives but don't either have a clue how to go about it, or if they have a clue, don't apply the principles of the "Law of Attraction." They tend to speak of wealth as something that is beyond there reach, something that's not available today or ever, and is only reserved for the very rich. People can recite a list of reasons why they can't have what they want in life. What they don't understand is they have the right to have what they want from life and rightfully so. They are limited only by their own perceptions and beliefs.

The techniques I am going to present in this chapter are very powerful in there ability manifest what you want in life. When you take these techniques to heart and with feeling and emotion you will become a magnet for the wealth and abundance. You draw to you that which you desire. It not just enough to just read about wealth or abundance you will need to change your thoughts, feelings, and your current actions to a state of mind called wealth consciousness.

Wealth consciousness is and awareness of the nature of the "Law of Attraction" and abundance, and how it flows. When you truly believe, think, and feel like a millionaire, you can become one.

As you work with the techniques in this chapter remember that the use of your positive emotions will fuel these techniques and manifest your dreams. Let yourself feel your emotions as you read and think about abundance and wealth creation in your life. You really need to take the time to absorb the material as you read it and take it to heart. As you read these techniques turn up the volume on your emotions if possible and drive these techniques home. When you take these techniques into your heart and repeat them over and over again in your mind, your conscious mind will convey them to your subconscious mind, and at that point your vibrational energy will move to a higher level. High vibrations attract what you want, low vibration repel what you want. High vibrations activate the positive side of "Law of Attraction" in your life. Once you have accomplished this the world is your pearl. Remember that you need to affirm you belief in what you want in life, not just hopeful wishes. The key is to move beyond merely reciting your affirmation and to truly believe in them.

Affirmations are positive declarations in the present tense, and because they are in the present tense, you are able to easily create the emotions necessary to attract abundance and wealth. You need to let the Universe know that you activating the "Law of Attraction" when it comes to your desires. Just saying "I wish I was rich" creates a feeling of lack and tells the Universe nothing. Now say to yourself, "I am wealthy," and truly believe in your and heart and mind that you are, the Universe will reciprocate.

What most people don't know or understand is that the subconscious mind doesn't have the ability to distinguish between reality and what you are imaging. If you hold a strong sense of abundance and wealth in your mind this sense will, at some point, make it to your subconscious mind and create the environment you need to attract whatever you were imaging.

Applying these Techniques

When a baby is born the baby sees the world upside down for the first three weeks and then, as if by magic, there vision inverts and they see the world right side up. Scientist discovered that it takes three weeks to develop a habit. So to begin attracting abundance and wealth in your life you will need to focus for 21 days on each technique present in this chapter. You only need to focus for a few minutes three to five times a day. The best time's to reinforce a habit, and plant this habit in your subconscious mind, is when you go to bed at night and when you first wake in the morning. At other times during the day find a place were you can be alone, if possible, and repeat your affirmation over and over again for the 21 day duration. Remember, when you finish reading a technique take time to affirm this technique in your mind and feel the emotion of this affirmation and affirm whatever you are attempting to attract.

First read all techniques from beginning to finish so you can get and understanding of what you are going to apply on a daily basis. Once your have completed reading these techniques, either write down the technique you are going to apply, or put this book next to your bed and read the technique first thing in the morning when you wake up, and also do the same just before you go to bed. After you read the technique write it out before your turn out the light and repeat your affirmation over and over again in your mind. This will convey your affirmation to your subconscious mind rapidly and activate the "Law of Attraction" that much quicker. Remember to truly listen to your words, out loud and in silence, that you are repeating to yourself. Feel the emotions and happiness of what you desire. This will raise your vibrational energy level to a higher state. Once in that higher state the Universe will respond more rapidly. Always remember, low vibrations repel, and high vibrations attract. As you go though each technique presented here take the time to envision each technique in your mind. Make it real to the point that you feel you could almost reach out and touch it.

Technique #1

You were Born Rich

What most people don't understand or believe is they have a birth right to be rich and have abundance in their lives. Just because a silver spoon was not put in your mouth at birth does not change this fact. You don't need a stack of $100 bills in front of you to be wealthy.

Wealth comes from within you, its and energy force that compels riches to move into our circle of living. Anybody can tap into this force anytime they like because it comes from a Divine source of abundance that is now and will always be available to us. Apply this force and you'll find that wealth will manifest itself in your life in several different ways.

The major reason why most people block the flow of wealth in their lives is they spend too much time on the details and how it will manifest. This blinds us and blocks us to the creativity that surrounds each and every one of us in the Universe. This blocking of our minds blocks the creativity of the Universe. We need to remember that the Universe is far more creative than we will ever be.

Money and jewels are symbols of wealth that we trade for other things of value. They are not wealth in and of themselves. Money is just specially designed cut green paper called currency. Jewels are just special pieces of rock cut and polished and sold for some dollar amount. Again, they are not wealth in and of themselves. Unless we value these items they become worthless to us. Abundance and wealth take many different forms for different people around the world. In the Middle East water is of great value, much more than many of things we value in America. What good would a TV do for tribes men in the desert? They have no electricity to run the TV, so the TV holds no value to them. In fact it would become a burden to carry around a 200 pound TV set with no use. See, no value. I personally place love as my most precious value far above the thinks I own.

Each person needs to realize they have their own hidden gold mine. Most people overlook the gifts that God has provided them. They spent much of their time focusing on their lack of things or money in their lives. Each of us needs to change our perspective on the way we look at wealth and abundance. We overlook our special gifts, resources, and qualities, whether it's our creativity, our ability to work hard, the love we bring to a relationship, our enthusiasm, or some other skill or quality that brings value to us and to the rest of the world. We need to stop thinking negatively about ourselves, the people we work with, our friends, the money and wealth we want and the world in general. You would be surprised how your own personal world would change if you just changed your thoughts from negative to positive. It would be like night and day. By changing your thought process in just this one critical area your whole life will change for the better. Negative thoughts will not allow the "Law of Attraction" to bring wealth and abundance into your life. You need to build daily on changing emotional patterns to a positive state, and when you do so these patterns will be conveyed to your subconscious mind and once this happens, as I stated earlier, the sky is the limit. Yes, abundance is and emotion and it is also a state of mind. Truly feel abundance and experience it and your eyes will be opened to all the abundance already present in your life. Then the "Law of Attraction" will be activated and bring more of the same. If you experience wealth more wealth will be brought into your life. When you have this experience of wealth, feel the emotion and when doing so your positive state of mind will send out high positive vibrational energy that activates the "Law of Attraction" and through the "Law of Attraction" will bring you more of the same.

Technique #1

You were Born Rich

Exercise:

1. Before you go to bed tonight write out what you desire or what you want to accomplish. Each morning, and at bed time, take out the piece of paper you wrote your affirmation on and reaffirm the desire or whatever your want to accomplish for 21 days. Also perform this affirmation during the day at least 3 to 5 times for at least 90 seconds. You will be amazed at what can happen.

Notes

Technique #2

Abundance – There is and Infinite Supply

The Universe is infinite, and there is an infinite supply of just about anything you can think of believe it or not. People today, thanks to the media, feel that there is a limited supply of just about everything, and do to this limited supply, they won't be able to gain access to what they want in life. Most people were taught not to be greedy and ask for what they want, but did it ever occur to you that the desire to have more doesn't always come from your greed? You may want more in your life so you can share your abundance with others.

When you are wealth conscious and give to the people you love and to the world around you the Universe will reciprocate and bring more wealth back to you. When you directly experience and become wealth conscious, truly believing that affluence is and ever-flowing stream that can be channeled and redirected through power of positive emotions and vibrational energy. What you will find is that you won't have feelings of greed or lack any longer. You will feel generous and giving as you wealth builds to and overflowing cup with abundance and joy.

When you hold the mentality of want or lack in your life instead of have wealth consciousness you will be fearful to spent you money because you don't think there is enough to go around.

What you will find out is that when you give freely and unconditionally, trusting that there is and infinite supply of abundance in the world, you will find that you will always have what you need to make it in life. Your rent will be paid you will have food on your table heat in your home and gas in your car or truck. When we share our love and give value to others from the bounty from within ourselves, the reverse will happen, the Universe will bring bounty back to use in such great measure, at times it will be more than you can handle.

When you become wealth conscious remember there are many ways to channel the flow of plenitude so that it rushes into the lives of the ones you love and the world at large. Buy a gift for a loved one, perform community work, set up a scholarship fund at a college or Christian school. Always take advantage of your ability to help others in need.

People tend to think they need a large sum of money to create wealth, but through the "Law of Attraction" this simply isn't true. It really dose not matter how much money you have at the moment because you can always grow more. Remember that there will always be "enough" for us and everyone else in this world. There are so many different ways for you to create wealth in you life. When I was a kid I took .45 cents and purchased three packages of Kool-Aid and opened a little stand on the corned of our street. That .45 cent investment was tuned in $5 dollars. You need to know that $5 dollars in 1968 was a lot of money for child to get his hands on. I took another .45 cents purchased another 3 packages of Kool-Aid and made another $5 dollars the next day. Through this lesson of reinvesting your profits to make more money I have built two successful IT businesses from the ground up, authored 6 books, consulted for some of the largest companies in the world, and hold three doctorate degrees. I found my inner Gold. You need to invest in yourself and the people around you and the "Law of Attraction" will reciprocate and bring your investments back to you 10 fold.

One of the best ways to build and create the feeling of affluence and wealth in you life is through visualization. Imagine lying in a beautiful green field, green is the color of fertility, and while lying in this field imagine the wind blowing O' so softly across your face. And within the wind is great wealth, breath this wealth in, breath in deeply, fill you lungs with abundance and prosperity. As you visualize this seen in you mind, your subconscious mind will pickup on these images, and once this has been accomplished your subconscious mind will go to work and activate the "Law of Attraction" in your life. You will need to repeat this visualization over and over again for 21 days to reinforce this image in your subconscious mind. But once this image has been conveyed to your subconscious mind, as I said earlier, the sky is the limit.

Hold the image or vision and the emotional sensation of drawing in wealth and abundance sending it outward with a positive emotional attitude. This will create positive vibrational energy being transmitted out to the Universe. Recite your affirmation as often as possible during the day and at night before you go to bed and first thing in the morning when you wake. Write down your affirmation as instructed in the previous technique. When and affirmation is written down it reinforces that affirmation in your conscious and in your subconscious mind. It turns the affirmation from a wish to a goal in your mind. The subconscious mind does not work on wishes very well, but a goal provides the fuel the subconscious mind needs to take action.

Technique #2

Abundance – There is an Infinite Supply

Exercise:

1.) As in the last exercise, before your go to bed tonight write out what you desire, be it a new car, Xbox, computer, love, wealth, or whatever your desire may be. Remember by writing down your desire you are reaffirming this desire into your subconscious mind. Then lie in bed and visualize your affirmation before your go to sleep. Take deep breaths in through you nose and breathe out through your mouth. Fill your lung with air, and imagine this air as your desire. Picture this desire filling your entire body.

2.) As often as possible repeat your desire throughout the day. If possible find a quite place were you can reaffirm your desire to yourself. Repeat and affirm your desire whenever and wherever you can if you can't find a quite place to perform this task.. Reaffirming your desire repeatability will convey this desire to your subconscious mind.

Notes

Technique #3

The Giving Universe

The Universe is always giving to those how ask. We are co-creators with the Universe. The Universe will respond to our request because it wants us to have all that we desire. The Universe has and unlimited supply of abundance and thankfully for our sake it is always giving. When we ask the Universe for something we need to put ourselves in the right position and willing to accept these gifts from the Universe. When we are putting out positive vibrational energy and feelings gratitude and abundance we put ourselves in that position to receive what the Universe has to offer. We become open to receiving.

As you go about your daily life you will realize that there is an enormous amount of wealth out there. Take the time to look around and see luxurious homes and expensive cars and think what it would be like to live in such a home or drive such a car. By creating these emotions within yourself you will activate the "Law of Attraction" and start drawing these items into your life. But only if you **TRULY** desire these items. Half hearted desires, and little or no emotional attachment to and item will not give off the positive emotional vibrations needed to attract these items or desire into your life.

Whenever you catch yourself looking at something and saying to yourself that it's to expensive, or I could never afford that, stop yourself and recognize that **YES** you have right to have this item or desire, whatever it may be. You have the right to enjoy prosperity. Step back and imagine owning that item, create the emotions and feelings that would go along with being in possession of this item, trust that the Universe will provide this item to you, or be blessed by some other riches in some way.

Remember the more positive your feelings are the more inspired you will be to grow abundance in your life. Through the "Law of Attraction" you will someday manifest that great sports car, or luxurious home, if that's what your desires are. The Universe always has these gifts available to you. It's your own negative emotions that block the Universe from providing all your needs no matter what they may be. Most people doubt that the Universe wants to bestow gifts and abundance upon them.

Try this experiment: Test drive a very nice sports car, visit the home of your dreams, take a walk though in a high end store you would not normally shop at. Create emotions of joy, happiness and gratitude as you perform these adventures. As you do this the "Law of Attraction" will start manifesting in your life. It may not be the very thing you were looking at, but some kind of abundance will start manifesting.

For many people creating the feeling of worthiness can be very hard, difficult and challenging. I was run over at the age of 10 by drunken drive and almost died. I wound up with one leg shorter than the other and became very self-conscious about my appearance. But thanks to my loving parents, and later in my life, my loving wife I was able to overcome these feeling of not deserving the people and things I wanted in life. I was able to build my self-esteem and through my new self-esteem was able to move forward in life. I now allow myself to deserve happiness, love and prosperity in all areas of my life. I know longer allow others to control the way I feel about myself. If someone criticized the way I walk, I step back and thank God that I can walk at all. The accident broke 60% of the bones in my body and I suffered massive internal injuries. It took many years and surgeries to heal my broken body. People need to stop judging themselves, and holding themselves up to someone else standards. More than likely another persons standards are wrong for the world and you anyway. People are so busy living in their own little world they rarely take time to see what is really going on around them, and if they do take the time, they are usually using tunnel vision to make there assumptions of what they see.

Technique #3

The Giving Universe

Exercise:

1.) At this very moment recollect a time when things were going very well in your life. Remember the feelings and emotions you had at the time. It could have been when you received the news that you were approved for your first car loan, or when you received that job offer you want so badly. Remember how tremendous you felt. Hold these feeling of abundance and well being as long as you can, and while you are holding these feeling focus on a new desire. A desire that you truly want to materialize in your life.

2.) Again as in previous exercises, write down this desire. Focus on it with all your might. Perform this task before your go to bed at night, and first thing when you wake in the morning. This is the best time to move this desire from your conscious mind to your subconscious mind, and in the process activate the "Law of Attraction." Repeat your focus on this desire 5 or more times days for 21 days, and hold the feelings of abundance and emotional gratitude related to having this item in your life. This process will signal the Universe of your desire and activate the "Law of Attraction."

Notes

Technique #4

Abundant Results through Infinite Patience

One of the key ingredients to activating the "Law of Attraction" in your life is being acknowledge and to value the abundance you have already created. By doing so you plant the seeds for future manifestation of abundance and wealth in the physical world around you. Remember that you reap what you sow, and if you don't plant you can't harvest.

Fear, lack, panic and multitude of other negative emotions will stop your ability to activate the "Law of Attraction." These emotions will change your polarity and cause you to repel, not attract, wealth and abundance in your life. You need to replace these fears with positive emotions, and through these positive emotions your vibrational energy will reset to a higher level and signal the Universe that you are ready to receive abundance and wealth. Remember that the Universe has its own timing as to when it will provide for your needs and wants, and if you hold positive emotions it will be only a matter of time before the physical world start to manifesting your needs and wants. But if you hold negative emotions, the Universe will be more than happy provide you more of the same.

You hold and emotional switch inside you, and once you flip that switch into the negative position and start worrying about when money will be coming you slam the breaks on the Universes ability to create positive results in your life. Wealth and abundance can come from many different places in this world. It can come through and unexpected raise or maybe you over paid on your taxes and didn't know that you did. The Universe has and infinite number of way to generate wealth and abundance in your life. For example, I filled out a rebate form for a purchase I had made and then totally forgot about the rebate. I had purchase a riding lawn mower and it came with a $100 rebate. Well it took 12 weeks to receive the check, but when the check finally arrived at my home I was not surprised. It was just that very morning that I was taking the time to release the emotions of abundance and gratitude for everything I have out into the Universe through my morning prays. Jesus said, "Ask and you shall receive, seek and your will find, knock and will be opened to you." Ask, seek and knock, and the Universe, which was create by the Lord, will provide you with riches beyond your belief.

People ask why we can't just simply hold positive emotions and send out high vibrational energy to create abundance and know without a doubt the exact amount of money that we need will be coming that precise day. What happens is we try to tell the Universe what to do and in our own terms. Quest what, it does not work that way, and you only find yourself frustrated and unhappy.

What you need to keep in mind is that often you won't be able to perceive that the Universe is working with perfect and unrelenting timing until after the fact, and you look back at the events as they unfolded. What you will find is that you did receive what you were asking for even though it may not have come in the form you expected. Let's use the rebate example from above: The same day my rebate check for $100 arrived in the mail my electric bill also arrived at the same time. I already had the money to pay my electric bill, but out of nowhere $100 arrived and I used that money to pay that bill. The Universe can be very creative in providing you abundance and wealth and this check arrived with perfect timing. This is just one example. I have seen this happen over and over again down through the years and not only to me, but to many other people. In many cases they didn't even know that they had activated that "Law of Attraction" they were just positive people by nature, and through this natural positive nature they were sending out high vibrational energy to the Universe attracting their desires. Again, remember whatever your thoughts are, positive or negative, and the vibrations that go along with those thoughts, the Universe will provided you more of the same every time without exception. The more you have faith in the Universe, God and the "Law of Attraction" the more your subconscious mind will go to work and draw your desires to you.

Why was I able to attract the money to pay this electric bill at the very time it arrived at my home? Because through the "Law of Attraction" the Universe was in alignment with my timing, I was in the habit of continually creating feeling of abundance in my life. If the rebate check had not arrived when it did I would have trusted the Universe and the "Law of Attraction" to manifest something better or at least different, but still some sort of abundance in my life. It's happened many times throughout my life. But a key thing to remember when manifesting your desire out to the Universe, which God created, don't be so emotionally dependent on having the Universe provide exactly what you want when you want it or you will block the Universe from operating according to it divine timing and wisdom.

As long as you continue sending out positive vibrational energy and working with the "Law of Attraction" you're going to be okay no matter what happens, so make sure you are open to how the Universe responds to your vibrations and you will receive the abundance you expect. Maybe not in the exact form you expected it in, but you receive abundance never the less. Never try to micro-manage the Universe it doesn't work, and only creates frustration on your part. If your desire is greater financial resources vibrate positive emotions and act in accordance with those emotions to create inner feelings of abundance and trust. When you do you will become and even greater money magnet and find yourself moving closer to your financial goals and desires.

When you have planted the seedlings of abundance and wealth leave no room for doubt and worry, because the Universe knows when to make the seedling take root and poke there heads through the soil and allow abundance to ripen to perfection.

Technique #4
Abundant Results through Infinite Patience

Exercise:

1. Create emotions of gratitude for all that you have even if you don't have all that your desire in your life, but affirm the desire that you do have. By creating the feeling that you already have abundance and prosperity in your life you will become a magnet for all your desires. Always remember the Universe has it's own timing, and it can't be pushed or rushed into manifesting your desires, so to gain "Abundant Results" you need "Infinite Patience."

Notes

Technique #5

You Don't need to know how – Just decide on WHAT!!!

The Universe has its own way of doing things. We as human beings tend to want to take charge of everything in our lives. We have difficulty trusting the Universe and its timing to provide and manifest our desires. When we try to micromanage the Universe and give instructions to the Universe on how to manifest wealth and abundance in our lives, we block the Universes wonderful and clever plans it has for us.

When activating the "Law of Attraction" in your life you don't need to know how the Universe will manifest wealth and abundance just that the Universe will respond and allow it to attend to the details. All you need to do is know what you want to manifest and create the positive feelings and vibrations and hold the experience that you already have what you desire.

Too many people assume that money is their only solution to their problems. Be open to the Universes ability to provide abundance in many different forms and many different ways. Always look for opportunities that will present themselves in your daily life.

People have the most amazing ideas, and just one can bring more wealth and abundance into your life than you can possibly imagine.

By allowing yourself to be open to the Universe and letting the creative juices to start flowing in your mind, your subconscious will start working on these ideas activating the "Law of Attraction" and the Universe will provide. Who knows, your idea may make you the next Warren Buffet (one of the richest men in the world). Many of the richest men and women in the world don't hold college degrees; I am not telling anyone not to go to college if you get the chance, but stating that just one good idea could turn into millions and even billions of dollars. Many people would say that it can't happen to them, well if you believe that way it won't. If you lock into your subconscious mind that you can't accomplish something your subconscious mind will not allow you to accomplish it. Also by locking this "can't" attitude into your subconscious mind you prevent the "Law of Attraction" from activating and allowing the Universe to provide for you. Moreover, don't get the thought stuck in your mind that the only way to obtain money is by exchanging a specific amount of work for a specific amount of money. You never know when and unexpected source of cash may show up in your life. You would be surprised at how many people receive cash that they weren't expecting. They just go out to there mailbox and out of nowhere there is a check for "X" amount of money. Be careful that the check is not part of some kind of scam. People have received checks that if you cash the check you just signed up for a year of some service and will be billed $49.95 a month for and entire year, so be careful. When these types of checks arrive they are not coming by you activating the positive side of the "Law of Attraction" or from the abundance of the Universe. If you are sending out negative vibrations to the Universe then the "Law of Attraction" could attract these types of checks. Remember that negative vibrations have a very low frequency and it take a long while to make the Universe respond to these vibrations. Positive vibrations have a much greater frequency output. The Universe responds to these higher vibrations much faster and provides more of the same.

What I have found down though the years is that many people have trouble or are uncomfortable receiving and accepting money for work they have not perform some kind of service for. Many people that receive unexpected money call the authorities and report it as suspicious and the authorities take the money and hold for some period of time or until someone claims it. Even after that period of time has past and the person receive the money back from the authorities they still feel uncomfortable about receiving money they have not earned. I believe most people would enjoy having the cash, but feel guilty because they have not earned the money, and they also realize that this is someone else's money and not theirs. I believe most people are basically honest and don't like to take what is not theirs. When you receive a windfall of cash or some type of abundance you need to emotionally accept this windfall, if not, you may put yourself in position that you repel this windfall through guilt or discomfort. If this happens you will lose that windfall 8 out 10 times and in many cases very quickly.

Always remember to rejoice in all the ways the Universe comes up with to give you the tings you desire in this life. Remember the old saying "Don't sweat the small stuff," keep this in mind when life attempts to through you a curve you didn't expect. To the best of your abilities know what you want in life and be open to how the Universe answers.

Technique #5

You Don't need to know how – Just decide on WHAT!!!

Exercise:

1. Three steps to manifesting and receiving what you want:

   A. Ask – Ask the Universe for what you want. Create and emotional connection to your desire. Visualize owning whatever this desire is. If it's a car, picture purchasing the car, driving it, and so forth.

   B. Respond - The Universe will respond. You need to do nothing. The Universe will always respond to anything you hold and emotional attachment too.

   C. Receive – You need to be open to receiving what the Universe is responding too. When the Universe manifest you need to be ready to receive.

Notes

Technique #6

Positive Emotions Increases the Flow of Abundance

Emotions play a large role in everything we do in life and *love* is the most powerful emotion of all. Even Jesus said "Love thy neighbor as thyself." Which means too love your neighbor as much as your love yourself (this is one view of the Bible passage). Love contains all the most powerful positive emotions to create abundance and wealth in your life. Most people that lack love in their lives also lack wealth and abundance. It's scary to think that people could go through their entire lives without loving someone or being loved by someone. Most people without love in their lives, but not all, lack even the basics of wealth and abundance building emotions and the vibrational energy to start creating this condition of wealth and abundance. But they are not stuck in this condition. All they need do, and its easier said than done, is to find something or someone in their lives to start giving love too, and their entire vibrational energy structure will change to the positive.

Love provides the illumination that removes the dark emotions from our lives and allows us to have further insights into our thoughts, actions, and feelings so that we can transform them into more loving ones. With love we can change negative emotions to positive ones and remove those feelings of lack, and create an emotional abundant state.

As we have learned in this book, up to this point, emotions such as fear, lack, and negative emotions actually create conditions that repel wealth and abundance, while positive emotions such as happiness, joy, and love promote condition that attract wealth and abundance into our lives.

That being said, you hold specific emotions within you that are especially productive in increasing wealth and abundance. As mentioned above, love is a very powerful emotion to create wealth, and another emotion to create wealth is the feeling of abundance. If you truly want to attract wealth into your life you need to feel that special feeling of abundance, and when you do these feelings and emotions will be transmitted to your subconscious mind, and once that happens your subconscious will work day and night to bring about the abundance you desire. The "Law of Attraction" works hand-in-hand with your subconscious desires not only with your conscious ones. Two of the key feelings tied to abundance is gratitude and thankfulness. When your conscious mind is full of the feelings of riches, you automatically are grateful for them which in turn activates the "Law of Attraction," and at the same time this grateful feeling is transmitted to your subconscious mind and it go's to work to bring more of the same. It is truly a domino effect from your mind to the "Law of Attraction" out to the Universe. Once this is put in motion there is no stopping it, unless you change your positive emotions to negative one.

Look around you and be grateful for all that you have in this world. Even of you don't own a lot of material possessions be thankful for your health, for your children, for something as simple as a sunny day. You can always find something to be grateful for in your life if you just look hard enough. As you cultivate the feelings of gratitude you will generate several other positive emotions, which in turn, will make you into a magnet for wealth, abundance, love, beauty, anything else you have come to desire in this life. Always remember that the Universe has unlimited abundance and is working with and through the "Law of Attraction" constantly. Negative emotions and fear distorts our thoughts and can cause us to overlook all the many God given blessing in our lives and all additional evidence that the Universe is providing for us and everyone around us.

Remember that the Universe runs on it own timetable with its own wisdom and plans. Once you make the positive emotional change from within, the Universe will begin to manifest situations and people that are in sync with your positive inner state and bring opportunities to build riches and abundance. When people work with the "Law of Attraction" they expect the Universe to respond to what they have asked for when they have asked for it. Well the Universe does not work that way and if you are expecting these kinds of results you are going to be let down almost every time. But when you give the Universe time and allow it to work on its own timetable you will be surprised at the abundance and riches it can and will provide.

Technique #6

Positive Emotions Increases the Flow of Abundance

Exercise:

1. Write down 10 things that you are grateful for in this life. Number them 1 through 10. If possible commit them to memory.

2. During the day and evening, at least 5 time total, take out the sheet of paper you wrote down the things you are grateful for. Read these items one at a time out loud and to yourself at least 21 times. Remember in and earlier chapter we discussed that it take 21 day to create a habit, well a same principle applies here. Continue this for 21 days and you will be surprised at your results.

Notes

Technique #7

Your Abundance and Your Beliefs

Your abundance is tied to your belief system and is in direct connection to the "Law of Attraction." You can become a money magnet if you want too. The stronger your emotion of abundance and wealth, the stronger you become a money magnet and don't think small. When you start thinking of your desires make yourself a powerful magnet for those desires. Vibrate enormous wealth and abundance and be willing to receive all that the Universe has to offer you. Don't sit back and say "I just want a little cheap car because that's realistic." Let the Universe bring into your life what it feels is realistic. If you decide you want a sports car create the feelings that you already own that car and don't block the Universe from allowing you to bring this desire into your existence.

What you believe to be true is what will manifest itself into you existence. If you believe it can't happen it won't every time. One way to start to manifest abundance into you life is to create a dream board. I have a dream board I keep in my home office. When I read a magazine and see something I want I cut the picture out and place it on my dream board. I of course I own the magazine first. Don't go cutting pictures out of magazines you don't own. This could be trouble. Dream boards are a great way to take what you see and convey this image to your subconscious mind. Once this is accomplished your subconscious mind will do whatever it takes to bring this desire into existence. Your subconscious mind will activate the "Law of Attraction" and manifest this desire. Another way to activate the "Law of Attraction" is look at the picture on your dream board close your eyes and hold this image in your minds eye. Really feel that your own whatever your desire is at that time. Connect your emotions to that desire as if it was already in your possession. Feel yourself shifting the gears on your new sports car, feel the wind blowing through your hair, and when you get up feel yourself putting the keys to your new sports car in your pocket. Make it real to your conscious and subconscious mind. At this point the "Law of Attraction" will have no choice but go to work on your desire.

Maybe your desire is for more money. Find a picture of a stack of cash and put onto your dream board. You might be surprised by how money can manifest itself at the very time you need it. Many times unexpected expenses occur in your life and when this happens we tend to focus on the negative instead of the positive. When we change our point of reference and focus on the positive, unexpected gifts and abundance arrive without notice from the Universe. I have found dream broads to be a very powerful tool in manifesting your desires. Another technique is to take those same pictures and place in locations around you home or office where you can see them on a regular basis. Put a picture on you dresser mirror, and one on you bathroom mirror. You may not realize that you are looking at these pictures but your subconscious mind is picking up these images every time, and once these images are in your subconscious it will go directly to work manifesting your desire through the "Law of Attraction" as long as nothing negative is tied to the image.

One of the key obstacles to feeling gratitude and abundance in your life, and I see many people struggle with this, is lingering resentment over past failures. Constantly playing these failures over and over in your mind blocks positive vibrational energy and in many instances totally blocks the Universe and the "Law of Attraction" from working in your life. One minute of positive emotional desire does not wipe out 8 hours of negative emotional contemplation. If you truly want the Universe to provide your desires you need to change your negative emotional system to a positive one. If you don't the Universe will not deliver what you desire. The Universe will deliver something, and most likely it will be something negative, and defiantly not what you desired. The Universe always delivers, so if you are constantly putting out negative vibrations you will get negative results, and if you are constantly putting out positive vibrations your results will be positive. That's the facts, and if you don't like them ask God change the Laws of the Universe. You won't be the first to ask God to do this.

Remember that whatever you have lost you can regain in some form through the power of positive emotions and positive vibrational energy. But this will only happen if you change your beliefs to a positive emotional output. Garbage in garbage out is always a good phrase to remember.

Technique #7

Your Abundance and Your Belief

Exercise:

1. Build yourself a dream board and put it in a location where you can see it on a regular basis. Cut pictures of your desires out of magazines news paper etc, and place them on you dream board. Remember to look at these picture often, and create and emotional connection to these items.

2. Take pictures of items you desire and place them on your mirror in your bathroom, and one on your bedroom mirror. Your subconscious mind will pickup on these images, once a positive emotional connection is made, activating the "Law of Attraction" and bring this or a similar desire into your life.

Notes

Technique #8

Abundance Language

The language of abundance is very powerful and can change what flows into your life from negative to positive and can also perform the reverse. When people's flow of abundance is restricted or abundance and wealth starts to move away from them they say something like "This happens every time!" or "Just when I am getting started!" or "Every time I get any money a bill arrives." You need to remember that when you validate a negative response to these life activities you are also validating the negative vibrations that go along with these emotions. When these emotion are negative and held long enough they will be conveyed to your subconscious mind and the "Law of Attraction" will start attracting more of the same.

You need to be very careful when making sweeping negative response about "always" or "every time" or "never" happens to you, and be conscious how you address and talk about "abundance," "wealth," and "money" and all the emotions that you create when you are thinking about wealth and the lack thereof. Take stock of your current situation but when you are thinking about or talking about abundance, wealth, and money, use language that sends a signal out to the Universe that you holding a new mindset a new way of thinking about these areas in your life.

Words hold a tremendous impact and the language you use to describe your abundance or lack thereof, actually creates the emotional energy and vibrations the effect your subconscious mind and the Universe.

Be careful of the words you choose to describe the different situations you are currently in. Take the two words "dead broke!" Yes, you may be in a situation were your bills are due and a surprise bill or two have appeared that you had not planned on, but are you "lifeless" laying on the ground "broken into pieces?" I would hope not! If you look around, you will find that 9 times out of 10 you have resources that you can make available to you. Use positive emotions, positive vibrations, and your subconscious mind to activate the "Law of Attraction" to create the wealth and abundance you need.

Most people feel that when they are in financial crisis or the brink of a major disaster that there is no way out, but they are wrong as long as you use the principles outlines here. If you use these principles you may be on the brink of prosperity and poised to turn your complete financial future around because you have finally reached the point were you have awoken and become aware of how you have been repelling money throughout you life. How people describe their financial situation, for better or worse, positive or negative, will actually effect their ability to change it.

Most people speak of money in negative manner, and many learned this from childhood. There parents held negative beliefs about wealth and past these beliefs onto there children. Parents tend to use the word "NO" when speaking about money. When a child ask for something in the store the parent says "NO!" and then continues to tell the child that they can't afford it! Now the child grows up associating the word "NO" with money and lack thereof. This also creates a connection in the child's mind that they should not ask or wish for what they want in life.

Parents should be very careful about the words they use to describe money and wealth around their children. Instead of saying, "That's to expensive" or "We can't afford that" the parent should re-phrase their words in such a way to guide there children to either understand why at that time they can't have the item they want, or if they can have the toy or game to explore why they would enjoy owning that item. This will reinforce the positive about owning something they want in life and not connecting the negative with spending money on and item.

If you are at a point in your life where you are facing financial issues, be honest with yourself about them, look into what resources you may have available to you and devise a plan to address and resolve your financial situation. By devising a plan you can start allowing positive emotions to enter your financial mindset which creates positive vibrational energy and in turn activates the "Law of Attraction."

Always use positive terms when thinking of wealth and abundance and what you want in life. Use positive emotional terms to affirm the things you desire and want to bring into your life and the lives of your love ones. Use words the instantly create a feeling of wealth and abundance and make them part of your daily vocabulary. Talk often about what you desire, and by doing so conveys these desire to your subconscious mind, which in turn activates the "Law of Attraction."

Technique #8

Abundance Language

Execrise:

1. Make a list of positive terms at least 20 that you can carry around in your pocket.

2. At least five times a day take out this list of positive terms and read through them. Perform this task for at least 21 days. I have been reading my list for years. Change and add to your list as events change in your life. This 21 day exercise will convey these terms to your subconscious mind, which in turn will activate the "Law of Attraction" to deliver more of the same.

Notes

Technique #9

Asking for what you WANT!!!

For many people asking for they want in life is as hard as pulling their own teeth. Jesus states in the bible "Ask and will be given to you," Knock and it will open," seek and you will find." This is not only great advice to live by, but it's the word of GOD so it's true. People tend to think this sounds too simple. But it's not! Many people hold on to their negative beliefs, and by doing so prevent them from "Asking and it will be given you." If you want something just **ASK** with feeling and emotion and the door will automatically be open to you.

Too many people today hold old negative belief instilled in them by there parents. They believe money is the root of all evil, or that people that have money are crooks or have done something evil to gain such wealth. Granted there such people in the world, but I know many wealthy and well-to-do people and they are neither crooks nor evil. In fact they spend a lot of their time helping others and donate large sums of money to various charities. Tearing other people down may make you feel better but it does not bring you any closer to wealth and abundance in your life. I have met so many people that believe that they need to sacrifice something good in their life to become wealthy and this is just not true.

One common fear is that they believe that to become wealthy they need to work 80 hours a week and sacrifice all their time in the pursuit of wealth and have no time left for their families or friends, or anything else for that matter. Again, quest what, they are wrong. I know of wealthy individuals that work only about 20 hours a week, and yes there are times when they need to put in long hours, but this not the norm for them. Also on the other hand, don't expect the world or the Universe to just hand you a million dollars for doing nothing. Yes there have been the lucky few that this has happened too, but don't expect it to happen to you. As with anything in life you will need to put the effort in to get the results out, and I am assuming the results you are looking for are abundance, love, health, and wealth.

Many beliefs are based on false assumptions. Many believe that to acquire wealth you need to be ruthless in business, and in many cases with the people around them. These false assumptions creates more grief in people's lives and in the lives of their loved ones. We need to change our thought processes to include the fact that you need not to be ruthless in dealing with others to obtain wealth in your life. It sounds easier said than done doesn't it. In the exercise at the end of the chapter I will introduce you to a technique to change your thought process in this and other areas.

Ask the Universe

Ask the Universe for what you WANT in life. Don't be afraid to go out and get "your fair share" of the wealth and abundance that's available in the world. Too many people hold the belief that there is only a limited amount things, money, or abundance in general in the world. Well I have news for them, the Universe has unlimited amount of wealth and abundance available to them if they just ASK!

Remember:

- Ask the Universe for what you want! Make and emotional connection to whatever you are asking for. Create feelings of ownership. Act and feel as if you already own whatever you are asking for from the Universe.
- Be open to receiving for whatever you have asked for. Being open to receiving is one of the hardest parts of the ASKING process for many people. They ask but don't feel worthy to receive what they have asked for. If you want to receive you have to change this mind set or you will not receive. Plain and simple.
- Now let the Universe do its part. If you have done your part, and have done it without greed, evil intention, or in a rush, the Universe will provide every time. It may not be the very exact thing you asked for, if not, it will be close or will benefit you in and even better way than you asked for.

Technique #9

Asking for what you WANT!!!

Exercise:

If you hold the belief that wealthy people are ruthless individuals and that you need to be ruthless to attain riches use this technique to help re-program your mind, and change your perspective on wealth.

- First, you need a tape recorder.
- Seconds, write a script that states that money and wealth are not evil, and that you need not be ruthless to obtain wealth, riches, and abundance. Make the script as least five minutes long. Say things like, "Money is good, I deserve to be wealthy, I deserve love, I am a good person, abundance and wealth comes to me easily, and so forth.
- Third, read this script into the tape recorder over and over again for about 45 to 60 minutes. I no this takes time, but it will be worth the effort.

Technique #9

Asking for what you WANT!!!

Exercise:

- Forth, start playing your recording each night just as you are starting to fall asleep. The purpose of this is; as you fall asleep and once you are asleep, this information will be conveyed directly to your subconscious mind. Once your subconscious mind has hold of this information it will go directly to work changing your beliefs about money and wealth.
- Fifth, make a second script asking for the items in the Universe that you truly want. Read the script over and over again for about 45 to 60 minutes into the tape recorder. Just as you did with your previous script.
- Sixth, read this script after you have finished reading your first script into the tape recorder so they daisy chain each other.
- Seventh, play these scripts for at least 21 days to form a habit out of them.

Another nice touch to add to your recordings is play pleasant music in the background as you read your script. Something soothing like waves crashing on the beach, or one I like to use is "Spirit Spa" by David R. Maracle. I picked this CD up at Wal-Mart in there Spirit Musical section near the candles.

Once you have completed this exercise for 21 days or more, you are going to be surprise at the results you obtain. These types of exercises have change people lives for the better, and there is a lot data out on the Internet to backup this technique.

Notes

Technique #10

Abundance of Resources

The Universe has large abundance of resources available to each and everyone on this planet and it's our right to gather as much or as little as we want. Each of us have many valuable resources to share with others, but all too often we overlook our own and others' riches, especially when they take on different or unexpected forms. When situation arise in our lives we tend to look at traditional forms of resources, and if these resources can't resolve this situation we don't know what to do next or where to go. Most of the time alternative resources are right in front of us, but since we are not use to looking for these alternative resources we tend to miss them.

In the event that we need to look for alternative resources to solve a situation we find ourselves in, we need to sit back and take stock of all our current resources that are available to us at that time. Even if we were to find ourselves without money, credit, not able to get a loan from a bank, most of us have someone who we can turn too, to help us out in some way if only we would get down off our self important pedestal and ask for their help. When a disaster happens here in the U.S. look at how complete strangers go to the aid of other complete strangers no questions ask. They send money, food, and even offer there own time and personal service to help others in need. People can be incredibly resourceful in finding ways to help and assist there fellow man or woman in times of trouble and need.

If you doubt your resources and feel that the wealth or abundance you need are limited, think about all the people in your life and what they have to offer you, and at the same time the resources you have offered them in the past. But don't look at what you have done for someone in the past as they owe you something. Always look at something you have done or the resource you have provided someone as a gift, never to be repaid, unless it's a loan and, and agreement has been reached for repayment.

Most people, when in need, they create negative feelings which leads to negative vibrational energy being sent out to the Universe. This negative energy blocks the Universe from bringing the right resources to your assistance to solve or resolve the situation you have found yourself in. There is no shame or weakness in asking for and accepting help from your parents, bother or sister, friend, or even your local church and community.

Most people don't realize that they have abundant resources all around them. If you want to invest in the stock market take some time and do a little research at the library, if you want to increase your management skills, again checkout some books on the topic from the library and read up on management. You can go out to the internet and find a world of resources and information to help you in just about any area of endeavor. A terrific way to become more conscious of your resources is to start tracking how you spend your money. When you start tracking where you money is going you will be surprised at what you spend you money on. I know I was. Once you have track this resource you will be put in position of re-channeling your money into investments that can over time make you very wealthy.

When you hold honor and respect for your resources that doesn't mean that the flow of abundance isn't necessarily predictable and isn't always completely in you control. In fact I have found that much of your resources, at times, can be beyond your control. It's not like standing in the middle of river that's forever streaming towards you and into your life. Sometimes your resource stream can be fast moving, sometimes it can be a trickle and sometimes it can even be moving away from you. When you resource stream is moving away it's usually because you are sending out negative vibrations to the Universe and blocking your flow of abundance.

When things happen in life, and I know at time it's very difficult, but you gain nothing by harboring negative emotions and feelings about whatever situation you find yourself in. Even during the depression of the late 1920's and 1930's there was a flow of abundance for those that new how to use the "Law of Attraction" and many became very prosperous during that time.

Always remember to nurture the abundance you have in your life, show and feel gratitude right now and let go of any attachment you may have to abundance that has flowed away from you life. Just say goodbye and move on. Once and area of abundance is gone it hardly ever returns, and if it does its not the same as it was before it left. Respecting your resources also means being careful and not being wasteful with those resources. If you see something and it holds no value for you save your money even if you can afford it.

Technique #10
Abundance of Resources

Exercise:

1. Make a list of the resources you have available to you.

    - Money
    - Home
    - Car
    - Investments (Stocks, Bonds, etc.)
    - Insurance (Whole Life)
    - Family
    - Friends

    Add any additional resources you can think of. Now, if at this time you need to access one of these resources do so. If not, keep this list in safe place so when you do need a resource you will have it ready and available.

2. Once you have completed your list, take some time to be grateful for all you have. This will remove many negative emotional feeling you may have, also remove any blockage you may have with the Universe's ability to provide for you.

Notes

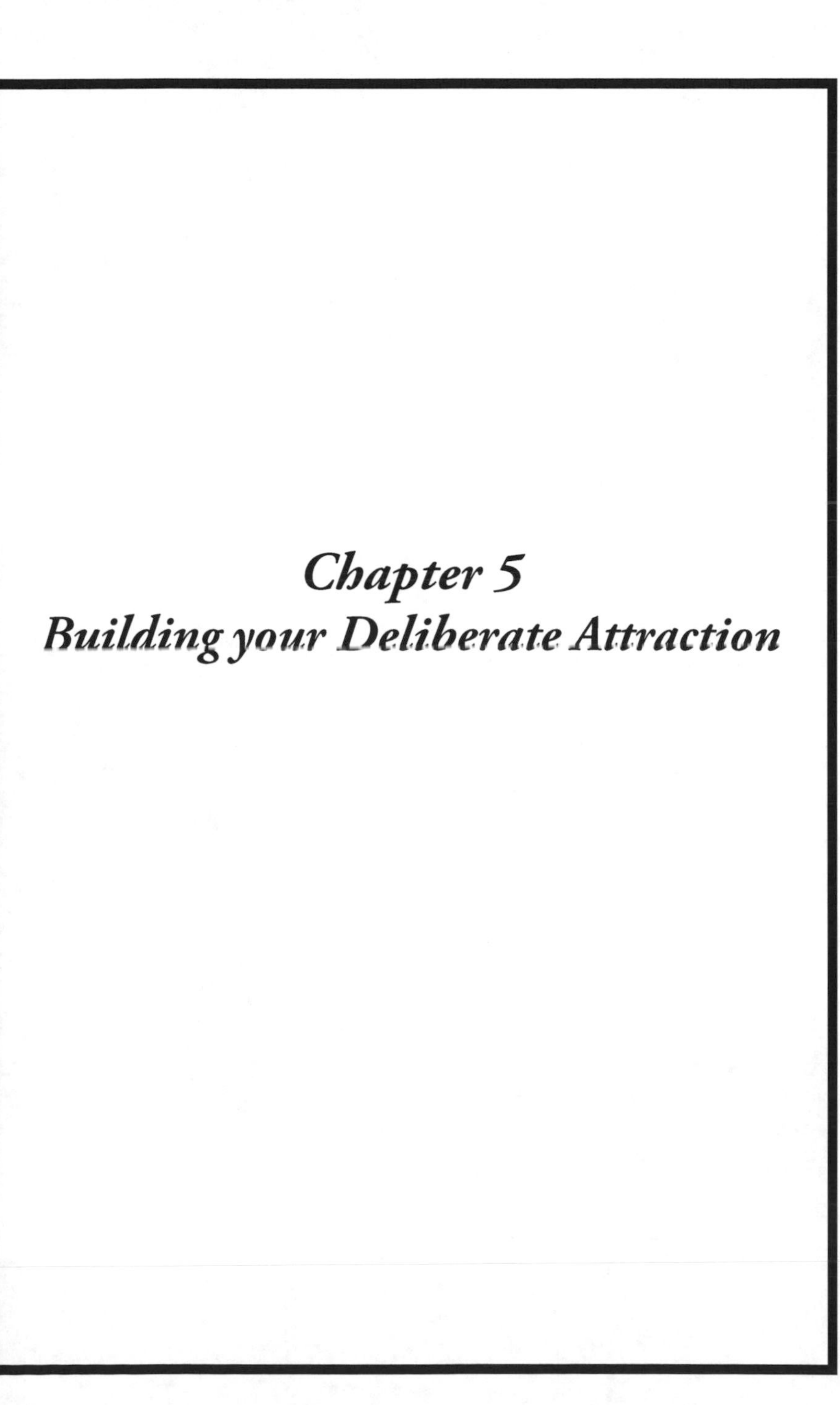

Chapter 5
Building your Deliberate Attraction

The following chapter will provide you with additional information on activating the "Law of Attraction" in your life. Most people don't even know if they are sending out positive or negative vibrational energy. One way is to simply look around you and your life, what results are you receiving in these different areas? This is perfect reflection of what your vibrational energy has been sending out to the Universe. People with bad attitudes tend to attract very little into their lives, and when this happens this puts them into and even worse disposition.

In this chapter we are going to discover additional techniques on how to use the "Law of Attraction more deliberately. We are going to use a 3-step formula which has been used for centuries by the people in the know. If you have seen the movie "The Secret" this is the process they were talking about. This attraction process is called "Deliberate Attraction." If you have not decided what specific areas of your life you would like to apply "Deliberate Attraction," too, just take a few minutes and think about the different areas in your life that you are least satisfied with. It could be in the areas of health, finance, career, personal relationships, etc.

3 STEPS

- Identify What your Desires ARE!
- Focus your Attention on your Desires!
- Allow these Desires to Manifest in your LIFE!

STEP 1 – Identify what your Desires ARE!

The "Law of Attraction" does not work on whimsical thoughts or ideas. You need to indentify what your desires are, and be clear about those desires. For most people this is a challenge because they are not sure what they truly want in life, but people are very good at knowing what they don't want from life. Knowing what you don't want does help in indentifying what you do want. Knowing what you don't want in life helps bring clarity into the good areas of your life where you do want better things to happen.

Perform the following task:

- Identify what makes your feel good?
- Make a list of these of feel good items?
- They can be anything you desire in life.

Through this exercise you will gain greater clarity on your desires and this will provide you with greater better ability to focus and activate "Deliberate Attraction." Remember we are only identifying are desires at this point not applying the "Law of Attraction" yet.

STEP 2 – Focus your Attention on your Desires!

Focusing your attention on your desires raises your vibrational energy. When in a positive mindset about your desires the vibrations you are generating create a positive attraction within the Universe. It is not just enough to identify your desires you need to generate positive emotions and feelings directly at those desires. Giving your desires positive attention ensures that you are including positive vibrations toward those desires.

When activating the "Law of Attraction" always remember that whatever you give your attention too, and focus on, the "Law of Attraction" will bring you more of the same. However, if you indentify what your desires are and don't give these desires the proper attention or focus then the Universe will not manifest these desires in your life.

Perform the following task:

- Key – Identify your desires.
- Give your attention and focus to your desire for at least 90 seconds 5 or more times a day for 21 days.
- Hold the desire for longer if possible.
- Attach your positive feelings and emotions to this desire.

As you continue to hold your attention on your desire you are now including the vibrational energy of that desire and aligning that desire with you current vibrational energy.

Remember, after identifying your list of desires keep them were you can either seem them or gain access to them on a regular and daily basis. The "Law of Attraction" and "Deliberate Attraction" can only respond to what you are giving you undivided attention to. You can't just let your imagination run wild and expect to activate the "Law of Attraction" it does not work that way.

When you take your desire and hold it for longer and longer periods of time they will be transmitted to your subconscious mind and thus in turn activates the "Law of Attraction." Remember that your subconscious mind is the key part of the "Law of Attraction" formula. This is what the other books on the "Law of Attraction" don't address and it's **key** to gaining what you want in life. Your conscious mind is to busy to stay focused on your desires for any length of time, that's why your subconscious mind is so vital in this process. No subconscious mind interaction, NO "Law of Attraction."

STEP 3 - Allow Your Desires to Manifest in your LIFE!

I know many of you will say "I have had desires in the past that I truly wanted and they never manifested in my life!" You need to remember that the "Law of Attraction" and "Deliberate Attraction" is a three step process. If you skip a step most likely you will not manifest your desires.

Now that you have indentified your desires, written them down, and given them your full complete and undivided attention. We are now ready to move on to step three in the process of "Deliberate Attraction" and this step is "ALLOWING."

When "Allowing" the Universe to answer your desires you are sending out positive vibrations and cancelling out any negative vibrations and doubt you had in the past about these desires. Allowing is the most important part of "Deliberate Attraction" process. Remember you need to remove any doubt surrounding your desires and beliefs or your will not attract it. The process of removing doubt is call "ALLOWING."

If you doubt you can have something you desire you are sending a message to your subconscious mind not to work on bringing this desire into your life. Doubt and negative vibration cancel out any positive vibration you have for that desire every time.

Therefore, you must remove all doubt about your desires before "ALLOWING" can occur. Allowing is the absence of negative vibrations and doubt.

Notes

Chapter 6
Additional Insight into the Subconscious Mind

What's a Goal?

In this chapter we will examine how the subconscious mind receives a goal and how this goal is acted upon. We will also provide some additional information about the subconscious mind ability on setting goals and accomplishing those goals.

First let's define what a goal is? According to Webster's Expanded Dictionary a goal is: "The point set to bound a race; a mark that players in some outdoor/indoor sport must attain; a success scored by reaching this; final purpose." I don't find this to be a very good explanation on explaining what a goal really is. What I have always understood a goal to be is:

- Something that you obtain either physically, mentally or both.
- Something that you can obtain at future date.
- Something that you reach for and not given to you.

I think the last bullet point holds the greatest meaning when thinking about goals. Too many people today want everything given to them. They don't want to work to obtain their goals. How can and individual build any self-worth and self-esteem if everything they have has been given them through no effort of their own. They gain know knowledge when given their desires. What fun is in that? You wind up with no accomplishment and nothing to show for your time here on earth.

The Subconscious Mind and Goals

As stated in earlier chapters the subconscious mind has it own way of doing business in conjunction to the outside world. The subconscious mind almost works in a dream state, and when you are asleep it does work in a dream state. Have you ever observed someone sleeping and seen there eyes moving under their eye lids? This is called "REM" sleep. "REM" stands for "Rapid Eye Movement. This is a point in your sleep cycle that you are in deep sleep, but by watching this person's eye (REM) movements you are observing the mind still at work. The mind never ever sleeps. Just like your heart never stops beating until your last breath. Good thing too, or you would be in world of hurt. Same go's for your brain, if it stopped functioning during the night you heart would stop pumping, you would stop breathing and the final result would be death. You're not going to reach your goals if this were to happen. Sleep also gives your brain time to rest and recharge for the day ahead. One of the key chemicals in the brain is serotonin, without this chemical in your brain you would go mad! During a person's sleep cycle serotonin is replenish throughout the night. Sun light, i.e. ultra violet rays, are also a key component in replenishing serotonin in the brain. (ser-o-toe-nin) is a Neurotransmitter that relays impulses between nerve cells (neurons) in the central nervous system. Functions thought to be regulated by nerve cells that utilize serotonin include mood and behavior, physical coordination, appetite, body temperature, memory, and sleep. As you see serotonin plays a key role in a human's ability to function. The reason behind providing you this information is for you to gain and additional understanding of how the brain works, and when this is understood you will have a greater insight in what make us as human's tick.

As we learned in the "10 Techniques to get what you WANT in Life" there are several ways to set goals and convey these goals to the subconscious mind. Goals provide the conscious and subconscious mind, for a lack of a better term, food for thought. The mind needs information to work with or it goes idle, and we all know that idle hands, i.e. mind, are for the devils work. The subconscious mind within you works continuously for the common good, reflecting an innate principle of harmony behind all things in your life. Your subconscious mind has its own way of doing things, its own will per se. It functions night and day, whether you will it or not, and through this "self-will" the goals you set in life will be worked on, again, night and day. This is a good thing because your conscious mind does not have the time or the ability to focus it efforts on and continues bases to obtaining your goals.

Well you have reached the end of this book, but not the end of this fascinating journey into the "Law of Attraction" and certainly not the journey into the unlimited abilities of your "subconscious mind." I wish the read of this book a wonderful continues life and wealth, health, joy, happiness, and love.

May GOD Bless,

Dr. Michael Williams